rainbo[w]

annual 1988

Gary Tilletts book

CONTENTS

Published in Great Britain by
World International Publishing Limited.
An Egmont Company,
Egmont House, PO Box 111, Great Ducie Street,
Manchester M60 3BL.
Printed in Italy by G. Canale & C. S.p.A. - Turin.
ISBN 7235 6807 3

WASHING DAY

"I can't find my painting box anywhere," says George.

Bungle is busy picking up clothes from the bedroom floor. "We are untidy," he says. "Look at all these clothes we've left lying on the floor."

"Here's another sock," says George.

"You'll have to carry it," says Bungle. His arms are full of clothes. "Look. I have too much to carry already."

"What a lot!" cries George. "Here's another sock."

"And some trousers."

"And a T-shirt."

"And another sock."

"That is a lot of clothes," agrees Bungle. "We'd better put them in the basket. If Geoffrey sees all this, he'll think we're very untidy."

"That's a good idea, Bungle," says George.

Together they pick up all the clothes. Clothes on the floor. Clothes on the bed. Clothes on the chair.

"There are clothes everywhere," says George.

"I didn't know we had so

many. There are so many I've lost count,'' says Bungle.

Just then Zippy comes in, carrying George's painting box. He looks at Bungle and George. Their arms are full of clothes. Lots of clothes.

''Hello,'' says Zippy. ''What are you two doing? Is it a game? Can I play?''

''We're picking up all the clothes,'' says Bungle.

''And it isn't a game,'' says George. ''It's hard work.''

''And you can join in and help,'' says Bungle.

Zippy looks round. Bungle and George have picked up all the clothes. There is nothing left for him to carry.

George sees something under the bed. It is yet another sock. Zippy picks it up.

''What do we do now?'' asks Zippy.

''Bungle says we're going to put them all in the washing basket,'' says George. ''Geoffrey will think we're untidy if we don't.''

''But we are untidy,'' says Zippy.

''Well, we must try to be tidy instead,'' says Bungle.

''If we put all our clothes in the basket, when we've

finished wearing them, it wouldn't be so much hard work.''

''What a good idea,'' says George.

At that moment Geoffrey comes into the bedroom. He sees Bungle and George with their arms full of clothes. Zippy is still holding one sock.

''You are good,'' says Geoffrey. ''I was just coming to get all that. I'm going to do the washing. It's good of you to help. Why don't you put it all back in the basket? It will be easier for me to carry. I won't drop things then.''

Bungle and George and Zippy put all the clothes in the washing basket. Geoffrey sees how full it is.

''What a lot of clothes,'' says Geoffrey.

''We said that,'' says George.

Geoffrey lifts the basket of washing to take it downstairs.

''Can we help?'' asks Bungle.

''Come downstairs then,'' says Geoffrey, ''and you can help me load the washing machine.''

The washing machine is in the kitchen. Geoffrey puts the washing basket down beside it.

Bungle and George and Zippy watch. Geoffrey looks at them.

''I want you to promise,'' he says, ''never to touch the washing machine if I'm not here.''

''We promise not to touch it, Geoffrey,'' say Bungle, George and Zippy.

''Good,'' says Geoffrey. ''Now remember that.''

He takes the lid off the basket. ''First of all,'' he says,

''we will take all the clothes out of the basket.''

Bungle, George and Zippy help Geoffrey to empty all the clothes onto the kitchen floor.

''There are too many different clothes to wash all at once,'' says Geoffrey. ''Help me to sort the clothes out into different piles.''

He looks at the big pile of clothes. There are blue clothes and red clothes. There are light clothes and dark clothes.

Geoffrey tells Bungle, George and Zippy to make one pile of all the light clothes and one pile of all the dark clothes. They sort them out into two piles.

''It's a good idea,'' says Geoffrey, ''not to mix light colours and dark colours together when you're washing.''

''Why, Geoffrey?'' asks George.

''Yes, why not put all the

clothes together?'' asks Bungle.

''It would be much faster,'' says Zippy.

''Well,'' says Geoffrey, ''you know when you use your paint box?''

''I like painting,'' says George.

''All those lovely colours,'' says Bungle.

''When you are painting,'' says Geoffrey, ''what happens when you mix one colour with another?''

''You make another colour,'' says Zippy.

''If I mix red and blue, I get purple,'' says George.

''And yellow and blue together make green,'' says Bungle.

''Washing is a bit like that,'' says Geoffrey. ''If I put a red shirt together with a white shirt, it can make the white shirt go pink.''

''Why, Geoffrey?'' asks Zippy.

''Because red is a dark colour and white is a light colour,'' says Geoffrey. ''If I put them together their colour might change.''

''So that's why we have one pile of clothes that is dark,'' says Bungle, ''and one pile of clothes that is light.''

''That's right, Bungle,'' says Geoffrey. ''First we'll wash the light clothes. Then we'll wash the dark clothes.''

''You are clever, Geoffrey,'' says George.

Geoffrey puts all the light coloured clothes in the washing machine. Bungle, George and Zippy watch him. Then he puts in the washing powder. Next, he turns on the washing machine.

The water swirls round inside the washing machine. The washing powder makes the water soapy. The soapy water cleans the clothes.

George likes watching the soap bubbles go round. The washing machine has a little window. They can see through it. A sock goes by.

''There's my sock!'' says Zippy.

At last, all the washing is done. Bungle, George and Zippy help Geoffrey put all the clean clothes out on the washing line. It is a sunny day and all the clothes will soon be dry.

The washing line is full. The clothes are many colours and they make a pretty picture.

George says he's going to find his painting box. ''I'm going to paint a picture of the washing on the line,'' he says.

''You'll have to use all the colours of the rainbow,'' says Geoffrey.

PICTURE BOOK

George, Zippy and Bungle like collecting pictures of different things. Geoffrey gives them each a scrap book, which is full of empty pages on which to stick things.

Some of the pictures are postcards. Others are cut from magazines and comics. Some of them are old Christmas and birthday cards. Each of them puts different kinds of pictures in their scrap books.

George likes to collect pictures of animals. He has pictures of a hedgehog, a lion and some ponies here.

Zippy likes to collect pictures of places. He has pictures of the seaside, a town and a forest.

Bungle likes to collect pictures of sport. He has pictures of a footballer, a tennis player and a racing car.

What kind of pictures do you like? Perhaps you would choose flowers, or your favourite cartoon characters, or even photographs of your friends.

All you need is a scrap book, some round–ended scissors and some paper glue to stick the pictures in with. Then you will be able to make your very own picture book.

If you wanted, you could make up your own stories about the pictures, and make it a story book as well.

MRS MACMOUSE

by Stanley Bates
Illustrated by Nicola Smee

Tucked into a corner, at the back of the garden shed, stood a large old fashioned doll's house, long, long forgotten. It looked very sad from the outside. The paint was peeling off, and even a few windows were missing.

But inside it was quite a different story . . .

It was full of hustle and bustle, comings and goings, squeaks and shrieks, from Mrs MacMouse and her enormous family. There were so many little mice scampering around that Mrs MacMouse lost count of just how many children she had.

There was Nibbler and Twitcher. There was Whiskers, Brownie, Short-Tail and Long-Tail. There were the two white twins with pink eyes, and no one could tell who was Whitecoat and who was Snowfur, not even their poor mother. And then there were Sandy, Pepper, Titch and Tracey.

Tracey was a funny name to give to a mouse, but one day Mrs MacMouse had heard someone outside shout "Tracey!" when she was scuttling past the dustbins, and thought she would call one of her children Tracey.

In the kitchen with Mrs MacMouse and her husband, who always seemed to be out and about looking for food, were the babies, but they hadn't been given names yet.

As the mice grew up they left home, and one day the doll's house was quite empty, except for Mrs MacMouse and her husband.

She was very lonely. It used to be such fun when the house was full, but now all the rooms were silent and shut. Mrs MacMouse and her husband stayed in the kitchen looking at each other, and the days seemed very long.

Then, one day, came a knock at the door. It was a family of Field Mice. The farmer had cut down the corn he was growing, so the poor Field Mice had no home.

"Come in, m'dears," said Mrs MacMouse. "You can have the big bedroom upstairs."

Next came two sleepy Dormice. Someone had broken the flower pot they lived in.

"You can have the small bedroom," Mrs MacMouse said.

Then some Town Mice arrived. They didn't like living in a town any more. "Too dirty," they said, and were given the loft.

Very soon the doll's house was full of mice again, and Mrs MacMouse was very happy.

"It's just like it used to be," she said to her husband, but he wasn't there. He was out and about again looking for food for their new family.

THE TOY CUPBOARD

Bungle, Zippy and George decide to tidy up their toy cupboard. They take everything out and put it all on the floor. Then they sort all the toys into groups ready to put back neatly on the shelves and in the drawers.

Can you help Bungle, Zippy and George count all the different toys? How many do they have of each?

Answers:

1 Spinning top
2 Paint boxes
3 Teddy bears
4 Jigsaws
5 Games
6 Cars
7 Coloured pencils
8 Books
9 Building bricks
10 Soldiers

MAKING MUSIC

George, Zippy and Bungle are watching a musical show on television. There are songs and music, and they all enjoy it very much.

Geoffrey comes in and sits down.

''I wish *we* could make music like that,'' says Zippy, ''but we don't have any musical instruments to play.''

''We can make some,'' says Geoffrey. ''It's easy. Look, I'll show you how.''

Geoffrey shows Zippy, George and Bungle how to make their own musical instruments out of odds and ends.

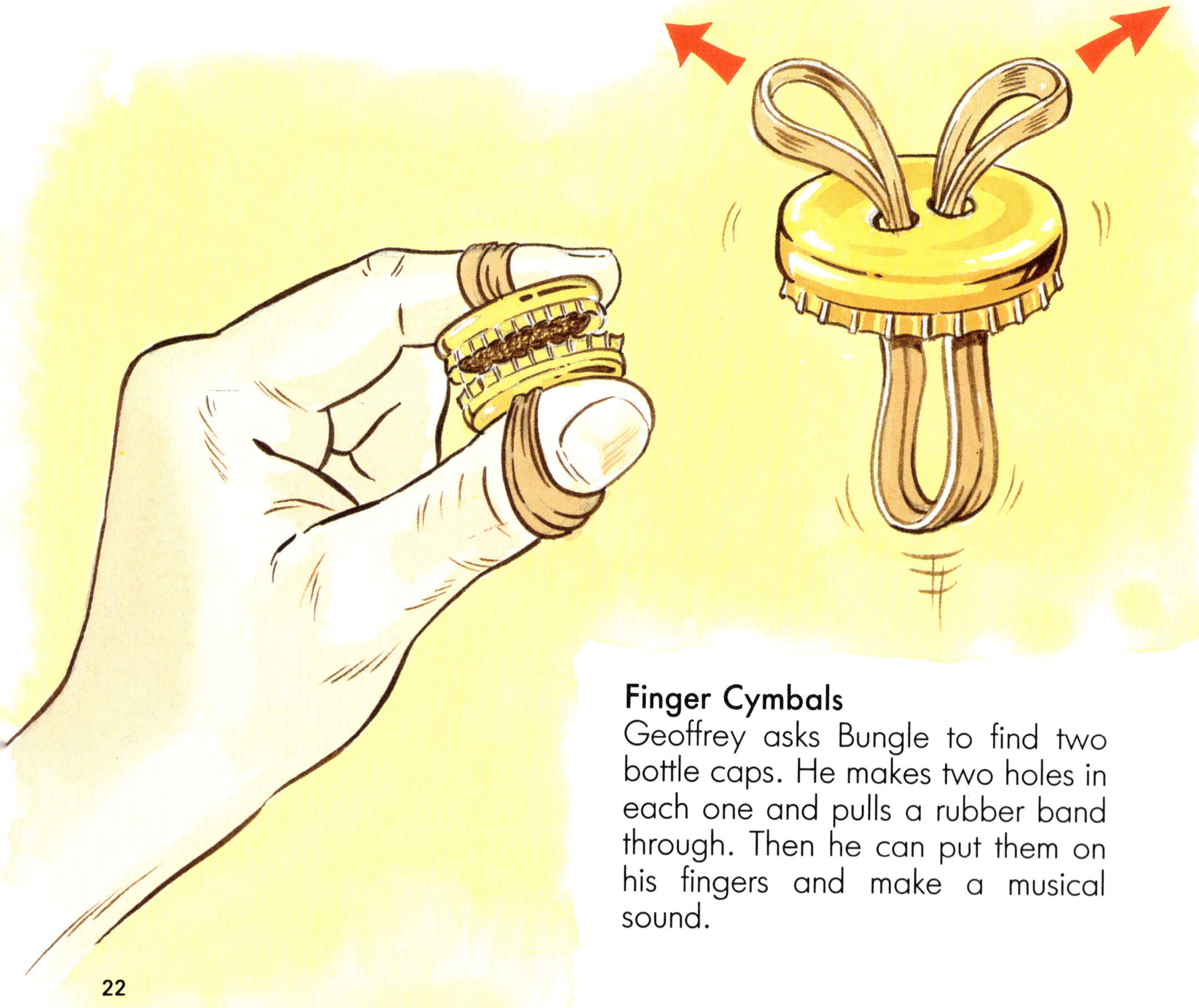

Finger Cymbals

Geoffrey asks Bungle to find two bottle caps. He makes two holes in each one and pulls a rubber band through. Then he can put them on his fingers and make a musical sound.

Rattle Shaker

Geoffrey asks George to find an old, clean yogurt pot, some dried peas and some Sellotape. He puts the peas in the pot and fastens the lid on. Then he sticks Sellotape all around the lid. Now he can make a rattling sound without the top flying off and the peas going everywhere.

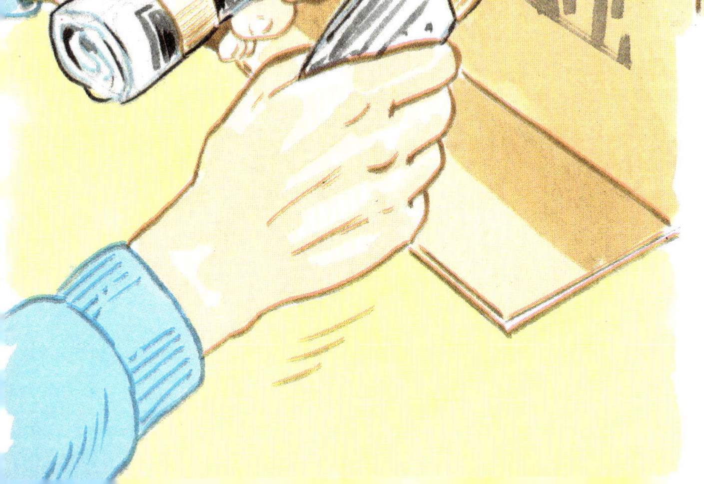

A Drum

Geoffrey asks Zippy to find a strong cardboard box and an old newspaper. He uses George's Sellotape to fasten two rolled newspaper drumsticks. He turns the box upside down and plays his drum.

A Rainbow Pinta Phone

Geoffrey makes himself a pinta phone. He finds eight empty milk bottles and fills them with different levels of water from low to high. He puts them in a line and taps each one to make eight notes from low to high.

Just for fun he uses a few drops of food colouring to make the water all different colours. Then he finds a wooden spoon to use to make the sounds.

Now that they have all the musical instruments, they decide to make up their own song to play and sing along to.

"What is a tune we all know?" asks Geoffrey.

Zippy, George and Bungle have a good think.

"I know a good one," says George. "It's called *Three Blind Mice.*"

"Oh, I know that one," says Bungle.

''So do I,'' says Zippy.

Geoffrey says it would be a good idea to try it out, all playing along and singing the words.

''I remember them, Geoffrey,'' says Bungle.

''All right,'' says Geoffrey. ''Sing the words to us.''

Bungle stands up, clears his throat and begins to sing. When he finishes, George, Zippy and Geoffrey all cheer because Bungle sings it very well.

''Can we all join in now?'' asks Zippy.

''Yes, and play the musical instruments,'' adds George.

''I'll have to practise it until I get the notes right,'' says Geoffrey. ''I know, while I do that why don't you three make up a song of your own?''

''Oh, we couldn't do that Geoffrey,'' says Zippy.

''No, we don't know how to make up songs,'' says Bungle.

Geoffrey explains how easy it is. Using the tune of *Three Blind Mice,* all Zippy, George and Bungle have to do is make up some new words to the same tune.

''What a good idea!'' says George.

Geoffrey writes out the words of *Three Blind Mice* on a big piece of paper for them all to see.

Bungle notices something strange about the words when he sees them written down.

"Look at that, Geoffrey," says Bungle. "Some of the words are the same – mice and mice, run and run."

Geoffrey underlines them on the piece of paper with his pencil. Then Zippy notices something else.

"Some of the words sound nearly the same," says Zippy. "Listen – wife, knife, life."

"Well done," says Geoffrey. "Those words are called rhymes – they are words that *sound* alike."

George, Zippy and Bungle decide to try and write their own rhymes to the tune, while Geoffrey learns how to play the tune on the rainbow pinta phone.

With all of them working together, it isn't long before they have made up their own song.

"We're ready," says Bungle.

"Are you ready, Geoffrey?" asks Zippy.

"Yes, I think so," says Geoffrey. "Do you all have your instruments ready?"

"Yes, Geoffrey," says Zippy. "I have my drum."

"And I have my rattle shaker," says George.

"And I have my finger cymbals," adds Bungle.

Geoffrey writes up the new words on the blackboard so they can all see them while they play and sing.

At last, they are all ready. When Geoffrey gives a nod they begin.

Three good friends, three good friends,
Singing a song, singing a song,
They all make music, just watch them play,
Singing and playing in their own way,
Did you ever hear such a sound as today
From three good friends.

At the end they all clap.
"That was fun, Geoffrey," says George.
"Yes, I enjoyed that," says Bungle.
"Can we do it again, Geoffrey?" asks Zippy.
Just then, Jane knocks at the door. Geoffrey invites her in. She sees that George, Bungle, Zippy and Geoffrey have musical instruments. She looks at the blackboard and sees the words of their song.
"Would you like to hear our song?" asks George.
"Oh, yes please," says Jane.
So George, Zippy, Bungle and Geoffrey play their song. Jane thinks it's lovely and claps very loudly.

DAYS OF THE WEEK

There are seven days in a week. Bungle, Zippy and George do something different every day. They decide to keep a diary and write down what they do each day of the week.

On MONDAY we help Geoffrey do the washing. We collect all our dirty clothes and put them in the washing machine. It washes them clean. Then we put them out to dry.

On TUESDAY we go with Geoffrey to the market. There are lots of different stalls at the market. Some sell fruit and vegetables, some sell clothes, and others sell pots and pans.

On WEDNESDAY Geoffrey takes us to visit Jane. We can play in Jane's garden. She has a swing. When tea is ready Jane and Geoffrey call us in. We wash our hands and sit down to eat.

On THURSDAY we all join in and clean the house. Geoffrey hoovers the carpet. Zippy dusts the furniture. Bungle washes the kitchen floor. George polishes the mirrors.

On FRIDAY we take a trip on a bus with Geoffrey. We buy some things at the shops in the village. We also visit the library and choose some new books for us to read at home.

On SATURDAY we like to go on an adventure. Geoffrey takes us to the park or the country. Sometimes we go to the zoo or to a jumble sale. Sometimes Jane comes too.

On SUNDAY we have a restful day. If it is sunny we go into the garden. If it is raining we stay indoors and draw pictures, or read stories, or play games.

SKY HIGH IDEA

Zippy, George and Bungle are talking to Geoffrey about the sun, the moon and the stars.

In the morning, when it is dawn, the sun comes up and lights up the sky. In the evening, when it is twilight, the sun goes down and the moon comes out. It is dark at night, but sometimes you can see by the light of the moon and the stars, although they are not as bright as the sun.

Geoffrey shows them how to make their own sky wheel. Perhaps you'd like to make one too. Here's what you do:

You'll need one big piece of paper and some cardboard the same size. You will also need some round–ended scissors, some paper glue, a paper fastener and some coloured pens or paints.

1. Stick the paper onto the cardboard.
2. Cut out two large circles the same size.
3. In one circle draw in the sun, the moon and the stars, just like the picture. Colour the sky – bright blue for the daytime, and dark blue for the night time.
4. On the other circle, draw a row of houses and trees, just over half way up. Cut along the outline.
5. Ask your Mummy or Daddy to make a hole in the centre of each circle, and put the paper fastener through the hole to join them together. Put the sky circle underneath.
6. Move the sky circle round to make a daytime scene or a night time scene. Watch the sun rise in the morning, and go down in the evening.

How to make a sky wheel.

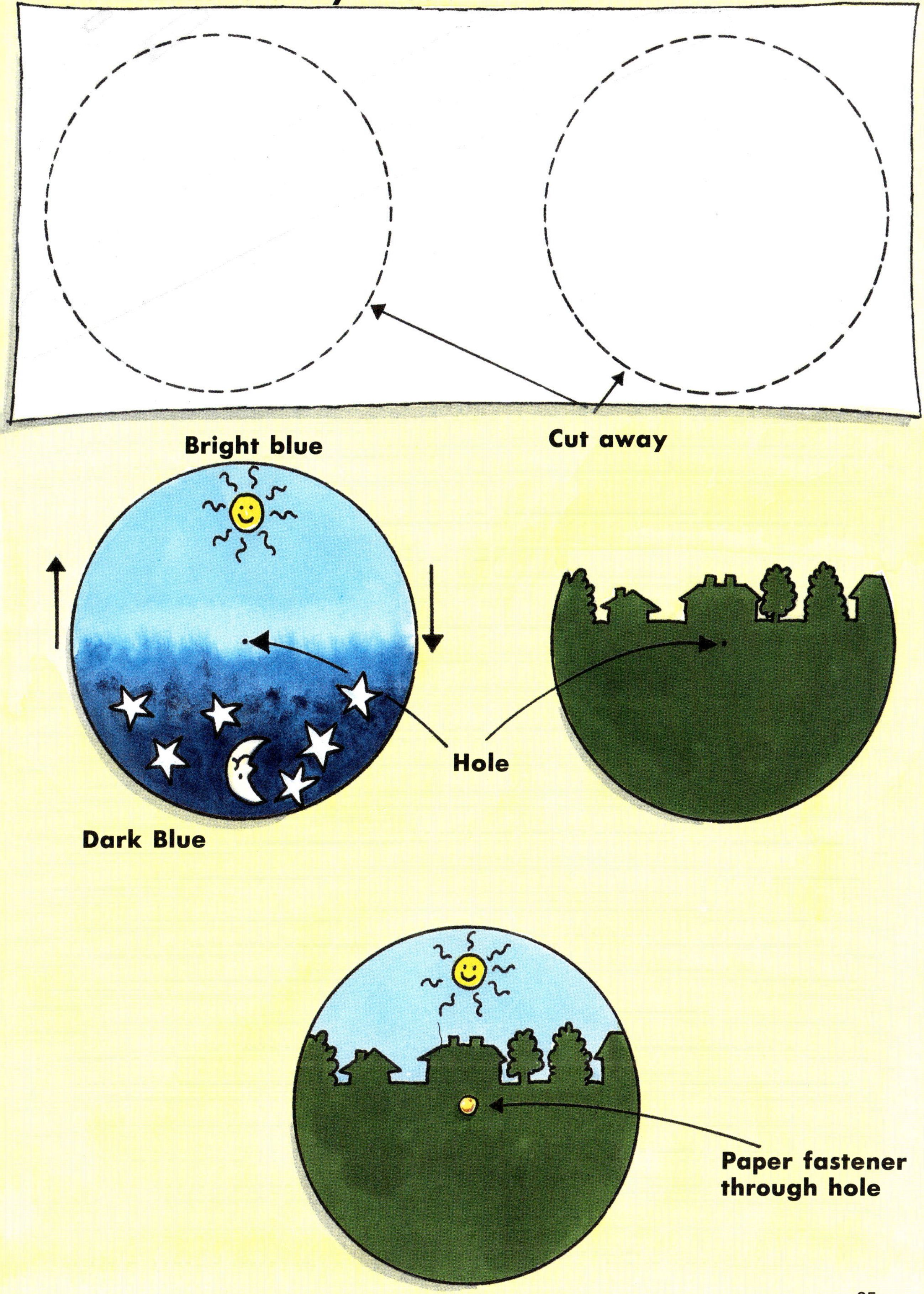

SUN, MOON AND STARS

Geoffrey shows Zippy, George and Bungle how to make themselves a mask. They make a sun, a moon, and a star.

First, he glues three sheets of paper onto some cardboard.

Then he draws a big sun on one, a big moon on another, and a big star on the last one.

Zippy, George and Bungle colour them in.

Next, Geoffrey cuts out the shapes. He makes two eyeholes in each one, to look through.

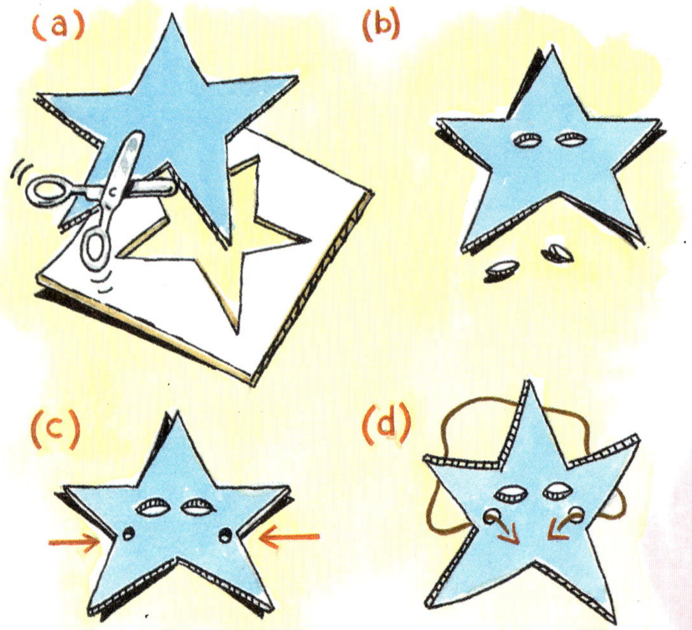

Then he makes two small holes, one on either side, and threads some elastic through. He makes a little knot at each end to hold it in place.

Zippy, George and Bungle choose one each to wear.

PETS' PARADE

It is early one sunny morning and George is still in bed.

''Come on, George! Wake up!''calls Bungle.

''Yes come on, George. It's today!'' adds Zippy.

George opens his eyes sleepily.

''Today?'' he asks, only half awake.

''Yes, Jane is going on holiday. We have to go and look after Jane's pets,'' says Bungle.

George's face peeps over the bedclothes. ''Oh yes, I had forgotten,'' he says.

''Well, come on then,'' says Bungle, walking towards the door. ''Hurry up and get ready. Geoffrey's taking us after breakfast.''

''Yes, breakfast,'' says Zippy. ''I'm hungry.''

''And if you're hungry,'' says Bungle, ''the animals will be, too. You wouldn't want to be kept waiting for your breakfast, would you?''

''I know I don't,'' says Zippy.

After washing, dressing and having breakfast, Bungle, Zippy and George are all ready to go.

''Is everybody ready?'' asks Geoffrey. ''Don't forget, we need to take some food for the pets.''

''I forgot,'' says George.

''I haven't,'' says Bungle.

''Nor have I,'' says Zippy. ''Look – there's some cake and a bottle of orange juice.''

''And I have got a jar of honey and some cheese sandwiches,'' says Bungle.

''Wait a minute,'' says Geoffrey. ''Do you remember what sort of pets Jane has?''

''I remember,'' says George with a big smile. ''She has a rabbit.''

''And a goldfish,'' says Bungle.

''And a budgerigar,'' says Zippy.

''A budgeriwhat?'' asks George.

''A budgerigar,'' says Geoffrey. ''It's a little bird with bright, coloured feathers. It's called a budgie, for short.''

''We know what pets Jane has!'' says Zippy. ''Let's go.''

''Wait a minute,'' says Geoffrey. ''Jane has a rabbit, a goldfish and a budgie. And you're taking cakes, orange juice, honey and some cheese sandwiches for them?''

''Yes. I like cakes,'' says Zippy.

''And I like honey,'' says Bungle.

''And I forgot,'' says George.

''Never mind, George,'' says Geoffrey, ''because we can't take cakes and orange juice and honey and cheese sandwiches.''

''Why not?'' ask Zippy, Bungle and George. ''They taste lovely.''

''Yes,'' says Geoffrey, ''I know you like them. But you're not a rabbit, or a goldfish, or a budgie, are you?''

''Don't be silly, Geoffrey,'' says George.

''Of course we're not,'' adds Zippy.

''You know we aren't,'' says Bungle.

''Exactly,'' says Geoffrey. ''What's good for you isn't good for all animals. Each animal has to have its own, proper food.''

Bungle, Zippy and George look puzzled.

"You mean rabbits don't like honey?" asks George.

"And fish don't like orange juice?" asks Bungle.

"And budgies don't like cheese?" asks Zippy.

"No, they don't," says Geoffrey. "And besides, you might make them poorly if you give them the wrong food."

"What do rabbits eat?" asks George.

"Well, a rabbit likes lettuce, carrots and oats," says Geoffrey.

"What do goldfish eat?" asks Bungle.

"Goldfish like special food that you can buy at the pet shop," says Geoffrey.

"And what do budgies eat?" asks Zippy.

"Budgies like certain seeds. You can buy those at a pet shop, too," says Geoffrey. "They quite like a little lettuce as well, and some cuttlefish."

"What's a scuttlefish, Geoffrey?" asks Zippy.

"A *cuttlefish* is a kind of shell that helps keep budgies healthy," he says. "Pet shops sell them."

"But we haven't any of those things, Geoffrey," says Bungle sadly.

"No," says Zippy. "We thought they'd like what we do."

"And I forgot," says George.

"It's all right," says Geoffrey. "I remembered. Look — I have everything we need in this bag."

And off they go to Jane's.

"Here's the rabbit," says George, "in his little home."

"A pet rabbit's home is called a hutch," says Geoffrey.

"A hutch," says George.

''Can I feed him now?''

''Yes,'' says Geoffrey. ''Open the cage door carefully, and bring his food dishes out.''

George takes the dishes out of the cage. ''There are two dishes, Geoffrey.''

''Yes,'' says Geoffrey. ''One for the oats, and the other for the water. Rabbits need fresh water to drink as well as something to eat.''

George puts some oats into one dish. He pours some water into the other. ''Where can I put the lettuce and carrot?''

''You can put those beside the dishes,'' says Geoffrey. ''Now put them in the hutch and remember to shut the door. Tomorrow we can clean the hutch out. We'll put some new straw down. The straw helps to keep the rabbit warm. And it keeps the hutch clean.''

''Can I feed the goldfish now, Geoffrey?'' asks Bungle.

"Yes, let's go and do that. The rabbit is enjoying its breakfast now."

Bungle soon finds the goldfish.

"That's a nice hutch," says Zippy.

"A goldfish doesn't live in a hutch, does it, Geoffrey?" says George.

"No, George. A goldfish lives in a bowl," says Geoffrey. "It lives in water. Just sprinkle a little food on the surface. Not too much though. A goldfish is only little so it only needs a little bit of food each day."

Bungle takes some fish food between his fingers and sprinkles it on the water. The goldfish swims up to the surface and eats some. "It's eating it," says Bungle. "Can we clean the goldfish bowl tomorrow, Geoffrey?"

"Yes, if you like," says Geoffrey. "We will need some fresh, cold water. We'll also need something to put the goldfish in while we change the water in its bowl. It needs to be in water to stay alive."

"What about the budgie?" asks Zippy. "It's my turn now."

Zippy shows the others where the budgie is.

"The budgie doesn't live in a bowl," says Zippy. "So this must be a hutch."

"No, Zippy. A budgie lives in a cage," says Geoffrey.

"A cage," says Zippy. "Where do I put the food? The budgie has no dishes."

"Yes it has," says Bungle. "Look, on the side of the cage. Here's one for the food."

"And here's another for water," says George.

Zippy puts some seeds and grain in the one for food and some fresh water in the other. The budgie begins to eat some seeds.

"Can we clean the cage tomorrow as well, Geoffrey?" asks Zippy. "We don't need straw or water. The cage has some newspaper at the bottom. We can use an old one from home."

"Yes, that can be your job tomorrow, Zippy," says Geoffrey. "Well, they've all had their food now. And I'm going to ask you to remind me to come back and feed them every day. We have to look after them until Jane comes back from holiday."

"Don't worry," says George, "I'll remember."

"So will I," says Zippy.

"Every day," says Bungle.

RAINBOW PATHWAY

Can you find your way round the Rainbow Pathway?
Here's what you have to do: beginning at the BLUE RECTANGLE you can move backwards, forwards, up, down or diagonally, but ONLY if the shape you move to is the SAME as the one you're on, or, if it's a different shape it must be the same COLOUR. See how many paths you can find!

START HERE

The winner is the person to take the least moves to return to the BLUE RECTANGLE you started on.

NATURE'S YEAR

SPRING

Spring is the time of the year when nature comes to life.

Everywhere flowers begin to grow and lots of trees start to turn green with all their new leaves. If you look closely you will see the little buds starting to appear.

Many animals have their babies now. Some animals, who go to sleep during the cold months of winter, wake up in the spring.

The weather is warmer, but it can still be misty in the mornings. There are often showers of rain as well, and sometimes thunder.

SUMMER

In the summer everything grows lush and plentiful.

There are very many flowers with beautiful colours and lovely scents. The trees and hedges are all green and bushy.

Animals love the summer, and if you look in your garden you will find all kinds of insects. If you watch the flowers you will see all the busy bees collecting nectar to make their honey.

The sun can be very hot in summer. It is a good time to go to the seaside. Lots of people go on holiday in the summer.

AUTUMN

Autumn is the time when nature begins to go to sleep.

The leaves on the trees turn brown and red and gold, and they fall to the ground. It's fun to run through a pile of leaves.

Animals start to grow their winter coats to keep warm. There is still a lot for them to eat though, because all the fruits and berries are ripe.

In autumn the weather turns colder and, like the animals, it is time for us to start wearing warmer clothes. The mornings can be foggy, and it rains more often.

WINTER

Winter marks the end of nature's year.

There aren't so many animals to see because, like us, most of them prefer to stay snug and warm in their little houses. Some animals go to sleep for the whole winter.

Winter is when the weather is coldest. Sometimes it snows and everywhere turns white. When it's very, very cold the water turns to ice.

Until spring comes once more, and nature's year starts all over again...

POOR OLD BUNGLE

Bungle is poorly. He has hurt his leg playing football and he can't walk properly on it. Geoffrey has sent for the doctor, and told Bungle he must stay in bed until he comes.

A little later the doctor calls and has a look at Bungle's leg. He tells Geoffrey that Bungle has pulled a muscle and that it will be rather painful for a little while. He tells Bungle he must stay in bed while the leg mends.

"Don't I have to take any medicine?" asks Bungle.

"Not this time," says the doctor. "The best way to make your leg better is to rest it for a few days. You don't need medicine for everything, you know."

After the doctor has gone, Geoffrey tells Zippy and George about Bungle's leg. He tells them that Bungle has to rest and not run about, so that his leg will get better more quickly.

"Does that mean he can't come out and play football, Geoffrey?" asks George.

"Not just yet, George," says Geoffrey. "First he has to give his body a chance to heal itself. Then he's allowed to practise walking on his leg to give it some exercise. Once it's all better he can run and jump as much as he likes. But it's no good him trying to do too much too soon, or he'll make it poorly again."

"Oh, poor old Bungle," says Zippy.

"Yes," says George. "What can *we* do to help, Geoffrey?"

"That's very kind of you, George," says Geoffrey.

"I'll help too," says Zippy.

Geoffrey explains that since Bungle has to stay in bed for a couple of days, they can help by taking him his meals and something to drink in bed.

"The best way you can help," says Geoffrey, "is to keep Bungle happy. It can be very boring when you're not allowed to get up and play..."

"...or go in the garden, or play football," says Zippy.

"Or go to the shops, or the park," adds George.

"That's right," says Geoffrey. "So it would be a very friendly thing to do if you'd go and play with him. Play some games, or read some stories, or do jigsaws, or colour in some pictures."

Geoffrey, Zippy and George are very kind to Bungle and look after him while he's poorly. Geoffrey cooks his breakfast, his dinner, his tea and his supper. Zippy and George take them to Bungle so he can eat them in bed.

And Zippy and George spend many hours with Bungle, keeping him happy and busy. Bungle's leg is soon very much better.

Geoffrey goes to see Bungle one morning.

"How are you today,

Bungle? Feeling better?'' asks Geoffrey. ''I think you can be allowed to get up today.''

''Oh, I don't know, Geoffrey,'' says Bungle. ''My leg still hurts a lot. I think I'd better stay in bed today and see if it gets any better.''

''All right,'' says Geoffrey.

All day Geoffrey, Zippy and George are busy looking after Bungle. First he wants a drink. Then he wants his comic to read. Then he feels hungry. By the end of the day Geoffrey, Zippy and George are all tired out.

''Do you think Bungle will be better soon?'' asks George.

''Because if he doesn't get better soon it's going to make *me* ill, I think,'' says Zippy with a big yawn.

''I'm sure he's almost better,'' says Geoffrey. ''Anyway, tomorrow's the day we planned to go to the zoo, so we can all have a day out anyway. If Bungle's still poorly, Jane will come and look after him while we're out.''

Next morning, Geoffrey calls in to see how Bungle is.

''Oh, I'm still poorly,'' says Bungle. ''I think I'll have to stay in bed again today.''

''What a shame!'' says Geoffrey. ''That means you can't come to the zoo with us. Never mind, Jane will look after you.''

A little later, when Geoffrey, Zippy and George are all ready to set off for the zoo, what a surprise! Bungle comes down, all dressed and with his coat on.

''Bungle!'' says Geoffrey. ''Are you better already?''

''Well,'' says Bungle a little sheepishly, ''I was all right yesterday, really, but it was *so* nice to have everyone do everything for me...''

''Oh Bungle, that's very unfair to your friends. We're here to help, not for you to take advantage of,'' says Geoffrey.

''I know, I'm sorry everyone. You've all been so kind,'' says Bungle. ''I'm sure it's helped me get better. But can I still come to the zoo, please?''

''Of course you can, Bungle,'' says Geoffrey. ''And now you're better Jane can come too!''

LEFT AND RIGHT

George finds it hard to remember which is his right hand and which is his left hand. Bungle and Zippy are helping him by showing him which is which. Can you help George as well?

1. Bungle is writing his name with his ________________ hand.

2. Zippy is holding his cup with his ________________ hand.

3. Zippy is opening the door with his ________________ hand.

4. Bungle is waving goodbye with his ________________ hand.

Which hand do you use to do these things?
Don't forget that Bungle and Zippy are facing you, so you have to put yourself in their place to find the answers.

Answers: 1. Right 2. Left 3. Left 4. Right

AT THE PANTOMIME

It is Christmas morning and Zippy, George and Bungle are unwrapping all their presents. Geoffrey has been given some presents too.

Geoffrey comes to a parcel that is all wrapped up in shiny paper and tied with a big bow. He looks at the label. It says:

Merry Christmas to Geoffrey
with love from
Zippy, George and Bungle

Geoffrey begins to unwrap it. He is very excited because he loves receiving presents. And he always finds that the unwrapping part is the most exciting bit of all.

"I wonder what it is," he says.

"It's a..." begins George.

"Sssh, don't tell him," says Bungle, "you'll spoil the surprise."

Finally Geoffrey takes off all the wrapping paper.

"We'll save that for another time," says Geoffrey. "Put it in the bag with the rest of the old wrapping paper, will you Zippy, please? Now, let's see what this is."

Geoffrey has been given a book by Zippy, George and Bungle. Geoffrey likes reading books, so it is just what he wants.

"Do you like it?" asks Zippy.

"We all chose it together," says George.

Geoffrey is busy looking through the book. It is full of stories and pictures. "It's lovely," he says. "A book of famous fairy stories. These are some of my favourites."

"We hoped so," says Bungle. "You're always reading us stories, so we thought you'd like a storybook of your own."

"That's very thoughtful of you all," says Geoffrey. "I used to read all these stories when I was a little boy. I shall enjoy reading them all again."

"Will you read them to us too?" asks George. "We like stories as well."

"Oh, George," says Bungle.

"It's Geoffrey's present, for him to read to himself."

Geoffrey smiles and gives George a friendly pat on the head. "Of course I will, George. Good stories are meant to be shared. Do you have a favourite?"

"Oh yes," says George. "I like *Jack and the Beanstalk*."

"And I like *Aladdin and his Magic Lamp*," says Zippy.

"Yes, and my favourite is *Snow White and the Seven Dwarfs*," adds Bungle.

Geoffrey begins to laugh. "I can see we shall have to read this book all the way through, won't we?"

George has a question. "Do *you* have a favourite, Geoffrey?"

"As a matter of fact I do," says Geoffrey, "and I was just going to tell you about a special Christmas surprise."

"What's that got to do with the book?" asks Zippy.

"Ssh, tell us what the surprise is, Geoffrey," says Bungle.

"Well," says Geoffrey, "my favourite fairy story is called *Cinderella,* and it so happens I've bought us four tickets to go and see the pantomime at the theatre."

"What's a pantomime, Geoffrey?" asks George.

"It's a story acted out on a stage," says Geoffrey.

"Like a play?" asks Bungle.

"That's right, Bungle," says Geoffrey, "but it has singing and dancing, and funny jokes and tricks. It's great fun."

Everyone is looking forward very much to going to the pantomime the next day. Geoffrey takes Zippy, George and Bungle on the bus into the town. The bus drops them off near to the theatre.

Outside the theatre there are long queues of people waiting to go in. Geoffrey has been clever and bought the tickets earlier, so they can go in straight away and sit down.

Inside, the theatre is very big, with rows and rows and rows of seats for the audience. All the seats face the stage, which has big red curtains drawn across it.

Soon the theatre is full of people. The orchestra, who play all the music, begin the first song. The curtains open, the lights go down and the show begins. It is the story of *Cinderella.*

Everyone has a lovely time. They cheer the singers, clap the dancers, and laugh at the funny men. It is all so colourful and such good fun that everybody leaves the theatre with a big smile on their face.

''Can we come and see a pantomime every week, Geoffrey?'' asks Zippy.

''They only have them at Christmas, I'm afraid,'' says Geoffrey.

Zippy, George and Bungle are very disappointed.

''But the theatres put on all sorts of plays all the year round,'' says Geoffrey. ''Perhaps we can choose one we'd all like to go and see soon.''

''Oh yes please!!!'' they all cry. ''That would be lovely!''

PANTO PEOPLE

If you go to see a pantomime at the theatre there are lots of different stories you might see. Here are some of them and the people you could meet.

CINDERELLA

This is a story about a girl who has two Ugly Sisters, who treat her cruelly. With the help of her Fairy Godmother, Cinderella goes to a ball. She meets Prince Charming, and he falls in love with her. She has to leave at midnight, but she drops one of her glass slippers. The Prince searches the kingdom for her. When he finds that the glass slipper fits Cinderella he asks her to marry him.

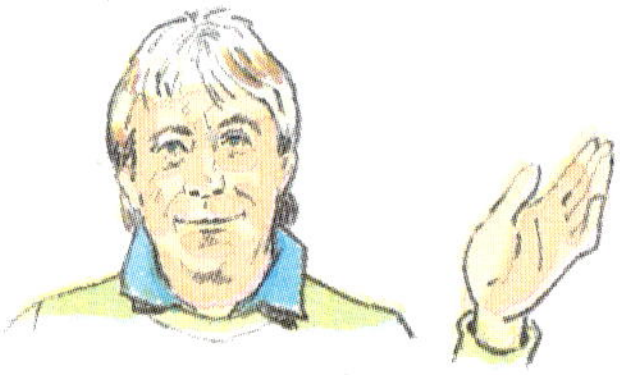

JACK AND THE BEANSTALK

Jack and his mother are very poor. Jack takes their cow to sell at the market. But on the way he swaps the cow for some magic beans. They grow into a tall beanstalk that goes up to a giant's castle. There, Jack finds a goose that lays golden eggs. The giant chases him, but Jack escapes and chops down the beanstalk. Now that they have the golden goose, Jack and his mother are no longer poor.

ALADDIN

Aladdin lives with his mother, Widow Twankey, a washer woman. His wicked Uncle Abanazar takes Aladdin to a secret cave to find treasure...but leaves him trapped inside. Aladdin finds a magic lamp. Inside the lamp there is a genie, who can make wishes come true. Aladdin marries a Princess. Abanazar steals the magic lamp and the Princess, but Aladdin defeats him in the end.

SNOW WHITE

Snow White is a beautiful girl. The Wicked Queen is jealous of her beauty and tries to have her killed. Snow White finds a safe home with seven dwarfs in the forest. The Wicked Queen finds out that Snow White is still alive and puts her into a deep sleep with a poisoned apple. Many years pass until a handsome Prince comes along and falls in love with Snow White. He wakes her with a kiss and Snow White and the Prince marry.

ADVENTURE IN PANTOLAND

A game for two players or more.

HOW TO PLAY:

You will need a die and four different coloured counters.
Each player chooses a pantomime character – Snow White, Cinderella, Aladdin or Jack. Throw the die to decide who goes first. Throw a six to start.

The first player to reach Old King Cole's castle, and land exactly on their coloured square, is the winner.